FOR LIZA

Copyright © 1991 by Cynthia Jabar

First Edition

ISBN 0-316-88884-2

A CIP catalogue record for this book is available from the British Library.

Joy Street Books are published by Little, Brown and Company (Inc.)

10 9 8 7 6 5 4 3 2 1

WOR

Published simultaneously in Canada by Little, Brown & Company (Canada) Limited
and in Great Britain by Little, Brown and Company (UK) Limited

Printed in the United States of America

# BORED BLUE?

## think what you can do!

### CYNTHIA JABAR

Little, Brown and Company
Boston Toronto London

When I'm bored
and when I'm blue,
I name the things I love to do.
Can you?

I love squishing-squashing in the mud,

kicking balls that end up, THUD!

raking leaves,

and swinging high,

little earth and great big sky!

I love making cabins out of wood,

riding through my neighbourhood,

mixing red and purple-pink,

skating on a skating rink.

I love cowboy hats,

and books galore,

go-go dancin' on the floor,

eating jam and buttered toast,

or scuba diving off the coast.

I'd love dining with the Queen of Crete,

tightrope walking without my feet,

surfing high on a sea of foam,

or travelling someplace far from home.

I'd love swimming in a chocolate sea,

climbing cliffs at Mount St. Pea,

riding carpets through the stars,

or jumping rope on planet Mars!

But now I'm tired.
What about you?
Name four things you love to do.
Can you?